God's High Calling for Women

God's High Calling for Women

by
John MacArthur, Jr.

MOODY PRESS
CHICAGO

ISBN: 0-8024-5308-2

1 2 3 4 5 6 7 Printing/LC/Year 91 90 89 88 87

Printed in the United States of America

Contents

These Bible studies are taken from messages delivered by Pastor-Teacher John MacArthur, Jr., at Grace Community Church in Panorama City, California. The recorded messages themselves may be purchased as a series or individually. Please request the current price list by writing to:

WORD OF GRACE COMMUNICATIONS
P.O. Box 4000
Panorama City, CA 91412

Or call the following toll-free number:
1-800-55-GRACE

1
God's High Calling for Women—Part 1

Outline

Introduction
A. The Situation Today
B. The Situation at Ephesus
  1. The occasion of Paul's writing
  2. The purposes of Paul's writing
    a) The topic of women
    b) The topic of worship

Lesson
I. The Appearance of Women (v. 9*a, c*)
  A. The General Pattern
    1. The meaning of "will"
    2. The meaning of "adorn"
    3. The meaning of "apparel"
  B. The Specific Problems
    1. Imitating their culture
      a) Juvenal
      b) Philo
      c) Pliny the Elder
    2. Flaunting their wealth
  C. The Proper Motives
    1. Of married women
    2. Of single women
II. The Attitude of Women (v. 9*b*)
  A. Godly Fear
  B. Self-Control
    1. The danger of failing to exercise self-control
      a) To the leaders
      b) To the congregations

(1) At Ephesus
(2) At Crete
(3) At Corinth
2. The judgment for failing to exercise self-control

Introduction

A. The Situation Today

The debate over the role of women in the church has reached massive proportions. Feminist philosophy has penetrated almost every area of our society and has recently made inroads into the church. I am amazed at how many evangelical churches, colleges, and seminaries have abandoned biblical truths they have held since their beginning. Books have been written affirming new "truth" regarding the role of women in the church. Scripture passages teaching the traditional roles of men and women have been re-interpreted. Some say these passages should be ignored altogether because they reflect Paul's anti-female bias. Others say these passages were added by later editors and do not reflect the intent of the original authors. The church, the bastion of the truth of God, is falling fast to the march of the feminist army.

The effort to overthrow the design of God for men and women is not ultimately a human effort. It is the effort of the archenemy of God, Satan, who uses sinful human agents to attain his goals. That's why the controversy over the role of women in the church is so tragic: the church is being deceived by the lies of Satan and is actually becoming a part of his attack. God has specific roles for men and women in society, the family, and the church that are clear in Scripture, and we need to re-affirm them.

In approaching this subject, I could take a lot of time demonstrating how far-reaching feminism is. However, it seems to me most helpful to simply look at the Word of God. If we understand what the Bible says, we will be able to deal with any error we might face. There is no passage more direct and comprehensive in addressing the role of women in the church than 1 Timothy 2:9-15.

B. The Situation at Ephesus

1. The occasion of Paul's writing

First Timothy is a letter from the apostle Paul to his son in the faith, his friend and co-laborer Timothy. Paul and Timothy met several years before the writing of this epistle during Paul's second missionary journey (Acts 16:1-5). When this letter was written, Paul had concluded his three missionary journeys and had just been released from his first imprisonment in Rome. After leaving prison, Paul met Timothy in Ephesus. Timothy was pastor of the Ephesian church. Apparently word had reached Paul that things in Ephesus were not as they should be. Paul had spent three years of his ministry in Ephesus and had poured his soul into that church. In Acts 20 Paul says to the Ephesian elders that he had not failed to declare the entire Word of God to the church but had warned them night and day for three years that error would come from the outside and that evil would rise from the inside (vv. 27-31). Unfortunately, his worst fears had come to pass: the church at Ephesus had fallen into doctrinal error and ungodly patterns of living. Most significantly, the leadership had been corrupted and needed to be replaced.

Paul personally dealt with two of the corrupt leaders, Hymenaeus and Alexander (1 Tim. 1:20). When Paul left for further ministry to the west, he left Timothy behind at Ephesus to straighten out the rest of the problems. Paul had been gone only a few weeks when he wrote this letter to Timothy to encourage him and give him directions for his ministry. First Timothy 3:14-15 gives the overall intent of the letter: "These things write I unto thee, hoping to come unto thee shortly; but if I tarry long, that thou mayest know how thou oughtest to behave thyself in the house of God, which is the church of the living God, the pillar and ground of the truth." First Timothy was written to set the church in order.

2. The purposes of Paul's writing

   a) The topic of women

   One of the problem areas in the church at Ephesus was the role of women. Since the leaders of the church had fallen into doctrinal and moral error, it's not surprising that there was a negative impact on the women as well as the men. First Timothy 5:6 tells us that some women had abandoned their purity and were living only for pleasure. Some younger widows had made promises to Christ to remain single, but they were in danger of violating them because of lust (vv. 11-12). Some had become idle, becoming talebearers and busybodies (v. 13). Some had already turned aside to follow Satan (v. 15). In 2 Timothy 3:6 Paul refers to these women as laden with lusts and easy prey for false teachers.

   b) The topic of worship

   First Timothy 2 focuses on another problem involving women. Under the pretense of coming to worship God, certain women were flaunting their beauty and desecrating the worship service. Their dress and demeanor betrayed an evil intent rather than a heart of worship.

   Worship is central to the church. It is not surprising that Paul discusses it early in his letter. In fact, it is the second topic he deals with in chapter 2, where he begins discussing problems in the church. The worship services at Ephesus were polluted by women who saw an opportunity to flaunt their wealth and beauty. Their sexual allure was drawing the focus away from the worship service. From his discussion of the problems women were causing in the worship services, Paul branched out into a discussion of the biblical role of women.

Lesson

I. THE APPEARANCE OF WOMEN (v. 9a, c)

"In like manner, also, that women adorn themselves in modest apparel . . . not with braided hair, or gold, or pearls, or costly array."

The phrase "in like manner" refers back to verse 8. It introduces a new subject related to the previous one. Paul now moves to a new topic within the overall subject of how men and women should conduct themselves in the worship service. "In like manner" serves as a transition between different topics within a broader discussion. It is used in 1 Timothy 3:8 to make a transition from the topic of elders to that of deacons and in verse 11 between deacons and deaconesses. Paul now moves from discussing the attitude of men in the worship service (v. 8) to that of women (vv. 9-15).

A. The General Pattern

1. The meaning of "will"

   The Greek word translated "will" in verse 8 (*boulomai*) refers to intent, purpose, determination, or command, in contrast to *thelo*, which indicates a wish. It could be translated "I command." It carries apostolic intent and divine authority. Paul is commanding men to pray and women to adorn themselves in a proper manner.

2. The meaning of "adorn"

   The Greek word *kosmeō* means "to arrange" or "to put in order." Paul is saying women should prepare themselves for worship. The Greek word translated "modest" (*kosmios*), the adjectival form of *kosmeō*, means "well-ordered" or "well-arranged."

3. The meaning of "apparel"

   The Greek word translated "apparel" in the King James Version does not refer only to clothing but can mean "demeanor" or "attitude." It encompasses a woman's

11

total preparation for worship, involving both the attitude of the heart and proper adornment on the outside. Her clothing should reflect a heart focused on God.

B. The Specific Problems

Paul not only gives a general exhortation about women's appearance but also deals with some specific issues that were problems in Ephesus.

1. Imitating their culture

Several ancient writers have described how women dressed in the Roman culture of Paul's day, which no doubt influenced the church at Ephesus.

a) Juvenal

The writings of Juvenal, a first-century Roman satirical poet, portray everyday life in the Roman Empire. In his sixth satire he describes women who are preoccupied with their appearance: "There is nothing that a woman will not permit herself to do, nothing that she deems shameful, and when she encircles her neck with green emeralds and fastens huge pearls to her elongated ears, so important is the business of beautification; so numerous are the tiers and stories piled one another on her head! In the meantime she pays no attention to her husband!"

b) Philo

Philo, a first-century Jewish Hellenistic philosopher, wrote *The Sacrifices of Cain and Abel*. He described therein a prostitute bedecked with a multitude of gold chains and bracelets, her hair dressed in elaborate braids, her eyes marked with pencil lines, her eyebrows smothered in paint, and her expensive clothes embroidered lavishly with flowers (19-21).

c) Pliny the Elder

First-century Roman historian Pliny the Elder told of Lollia Paulina, one-time wife of the Roman Emperor

Caligula, who owned a dress worth more than a million dollars by today's standards. It was covered with emeralds and pearls, and Lollia carried receipts with her proving its value (*Natural History* 9.58).

In contrast to Roman society, the mystery religions of Greece had stringent rules about the appearance of women. One inscription illustrates their concern: "A consecrated woman shall not have gold ornaments, nor rouge, nor face whitening, nor a head-band, nor braided hair, nor shoes, except those made of felt or of the skins of sacrificed animals" (cited in William Barclay's *The Letters to Timothy, Titus, and Philemon*, rev. ed. [Philadelphia: Westminster, 1975], pp. 67-68).

Both Paul and Timothy were concerned that the Ephesian church be a godly testimony to society. For the women of the church to imitate the gaudy clothing styles of pagan women, to call attention to themselves, or to dress to lure men into illicit sexual relationships was to blaspheme the intent of the worship service.

2. Flaunting their wealth

In the first century poverty was widespread. The wealthy could dress in a style that was impossible for the poor to match. Today, good clothing is relatively affordable in Western society. But in New Testament times, a dress worn by a wealthy woman could cost up to 7,000 denarii (one denarius equaled a day's wage for the average laborer). When a wealthy woman entered the worship service wearing an expensive dress, she caused a sensation that disrupted the service.

In addition to expensive dresses, rich women also displayed their wealth through elaborate hairstyles woven with expensive jewels (which is the meaning of "braided hair" in v. 9). They also wore gold rings and earrings and hung gold on their sandals and dresses.

It should be noted that the Bible does not forbid women to braid their hair or to own gold, pearls, and fine clothes. Both the bride of Solomon (Song of Sol. 1:10) and the woman described in Proverbs 31:22 owned expensive apparel. However, the Bible does forbid wearing those things for wrong motives.

Seductresses in the Church

After preaching a sermon a while ago I walked out the door of the sanctuary and was approached by a woman who was not appropriately attired for church. She handed me an expensive piece of jewelry, a gold chain, and a note soliciting me. That is an overt example, but there are many more subtle solicitations that go on in the church. Anyone who doesn't realize that has his head in the sand. Look at the many pastors who fall prey to sexual sin and the many churches that have to deal with immorality. That is one of the reasons for Paul's strong words in 1 Timothy 2:9-10.

Bringing down the Curtain on the Fashion Show in the Church

John Chrysostom, a fourth-century church Father, wrote this in his homily on 1 Timothy concerning the importance of women's dressing modestly for the worship service: "What is this 'modest apparel'? Such attire as covers them completely, and decently, and not with superfluous ornaments for the one is becoming, the other is not. What? Dost thou approach God to pray with broidered hair and ornaments of gold? Art thou come to a dance? to a marriage? to a gay procession? There such . . . costly garments, had been seasonable; here not one of them is wanted. Thou art come to pray, to supplicate for pardon of thy sins, to plead for thine offenses, beseeching the Lord, and hoping to render Him propitious to thee. . . . Away with such hypocrisy!"

The church is a place for worship, not a show. It bothers me when I see people who claim to be Christians preoccupied with their appearance. Whenever people use the worship service to call attention to themselves, it brings great tragedy to the church.

C. The Proper Motives

1. Of married women

   A Christian wife should attract attention to her godly
   character, not to her clothing. She should show by her
   dress and demeanor her love and devotion to her husband. She should demonstrate a humble heart committed to worshiping God.

2. Of single women

   Single women should realize that the worship service
   isn't the place to try to attract men. They too should understand it is more important that someone be attracted
   to their godly character rather than to their outward
   appearance.

How can both married and single women know that they
are dressed properly for the worship service? By examining
their motives. A woman should ask herself, *Why am I
dressed the way I am? What is my goal? Am I trying to draw attention to God or to myself? Will what I'm wearing stand out, or
will it be considered appropriate for the occasion?*

First Peter 3:3-4 is a parallel passage to 1 Timothy 2:9-10.
Peter writes, "Whose adorning, let it not be that outward
adorning of braiding the hair, and of wearing of gold, or of
putting on of apparel, but let it be the hidden man of the
heart in that which is not corruptible, even the ornament of
a meek and quiet spirit, which is in the sight of God of
great price." Like Paul, Peter emphasized that a woman is
not to be preoccupied with what she wears but with who
she is.

II. THE ATTITUDE OF WOMEN (v. 9*b*)

"With godly fear and sobriety."

A. Godly Fear

The Greek word translated "godly fear" (*aidōs*) refers to
modesty mixed with humility. It connotes a sense of
shame—not shame in being a woman but shame in inciting

lust or distracting others from proper worship of God. A woman with a proper sense of shame will not dress to be a source of temptation. *Aidōs* implies morally rejecting anything dishonorable to God. A woman who is grieved over the possibility of offending God will not do anything to cause someone to stumble.

B. Self-Control

"Sobriety" (Gk., *sōphrosunē*) is better translated "self-control." In extrabiblical literature, *sōphrosunē* is used to speak of totally controlling one's sexual passions and desires. In *The Republic* Plato says it is one of the four cardinal virtues.

1. The danger of failing to exercise self-control

   a) To the leaders

   In 1 Timothy 3 Paul says that both elders and deacons in the church must be "the husband of one wife" (vv. 2, 12). That phrase can be literally translated as "a one-woman man." A man in a leadership role in the church must be totally devoted to his wife. I believe one of the major problems at Ephesus was that the men were not faithful to their wives. Satan attacked the church by bringing alluring women into the church to seduce the men. And he does the same thing today.

   b) To the congregations

   (1) At Ephesus

   In 1 Timothy 5:14 Paul stresses the importance of younger widows remarrying. Paul knew that single women with strong desires for marriage were a potential danger to the purity of the church. And that's true in our day, too.

   (2) At Crete

   In Titus 2:4-5 Paul instructs Titus that older women are to teach young women "to be sober minded, to love their husbands, to love their children, to be discreet, chaste, keepers at home, good, obedient to their own husbands, that the Word of God be not blasphemed." Instead of doing good, some women were causing problems in the congregation.

(3) At Corinth

In 1 Corinthians 5 Paul rebukes the Corinthians for tolerating a situation involving sexual sin. The sexual sin was a form of incest: a man having an affair with his father's wife (his stepmother). Instead of mourning over that sin, the Corinthians were boasting about it (v. 2). According to 1 Corinthians 6:13 they attempted to justify it by quoting what was perhaps a common Greek proverb: "Foods for the body and the body for foods." That is to say that sex, like eating, is merely a biological function. But Paul warned the Corinthians to flee from sexual sin (v. 18). I believe that the problem concerning women with improper motives plagued the church at Corinth as well as the churches in Ephesus and Crete.

2. The judgment for failing to exercise self-control

In Isaiah 3:16-26 God pronounces judgment on women who dress to draw attention to themselves: "The Lord saith, Because the daughters of Zion are haughty, and walk with stretched forth necks and wanton eyes, walking and mincing as they go, and making a tinkling with their feet; therefore the Lord will smite with a scab the crown of the head of the daughters of Zion, and the Lord will uncover their secret parts. In that day the Lord will take away the bravery of their tinkling anklets, and their headbands, and their crescents like the moon, the pendants, and the bracelets, and the veils, the headdresses, and the armlets, and the sashes, and the perfume boxes, and the amulets, the rings, and nose rings, the festival robes, and the mantles, and the cloaks, and the handbags, the hand mirrors, and the linen wrappers, and the turbans, and the veils. And it shall come to pass, that instead of sweet fragrance there shall be rottenness; and instead of a girdle, a rope; and instead

of well set hair, baldness; and instead of a robe, a gird-
ing of sackcloth; and branding instead of beauty. Thy
men shall fall by the sword, and thy mighty in the war.
And her gates shall lament and mourn; and she being
desolate shall sit upon the ground."

Wearing jewelry or expensive clothes is not evil, but
wearing them for evil purposes is. Clothing that reflects
impure motives has no place in the church.

Focusing on the Facts

1. Who is behind the attack on the God-designed roles for men
   and women (see p. 8)?
2. Describe the circumstances that prompted Paul to write 1 Timothy (see p. 9).
3. What was Paul's main purpose in writing 1 Timothy (3:14-15,
   see p. 9)?
4. What were some of the problems involving the women in the
   Ephesian church (see p. 10)?
5. What is the significance of the phrase "in like manner" in verse
   9 (see p. 11)?
6. Describe the cultural setting in which the Ephesian church
   found itself regarding women's clothing (see pp. 12-13).
7. True or false: According to the Bible, it is always wrong for
   women to wear expensive jewelry and clothes (see pp. 13-14).
8. How can a woman know if she is properly dressed to attend
   the worship service (see p. 15)?
9. A woman is not to be preoccupied with _____ _____
   _____ but _____ _____ _____ (see p. 15).
10. What should be a woman's attitude toward distracting some-
    one from worshiping God (see p. 15)?
11. Why might Paul have included "husband of one wife" as one
    of the qualifications for church leaders (see p. 16)?
12. How did the Corinthians defend their toleration of sexual sin
    (cf. 1 Cor. 6:13; see p. 17)?
13. What is Paul's counsel on how to avoid sexual sin (cf. 1 Cor.
    6:18; see p. 17)?

Pondering the Principles

1. First Timothy 2:9 stresses the importance of preparing for the worship service. When you go to church, the issue is not just how well prepared the preacher or the choir is but how well *you* are prepared to worship God. As you prepare for the worship service, ask yourself: *Am I sincere? Is my attention focused on God? Am I coming to worship God knowing His acceptance of me is based solely on what Christ has done for me? Am I coming with a pure heart, having dealt with any sin in my life? Am I coming to be a spectator or a participant?*

2. Although 1 Timothy 2:9 teaches the importance of women's attitudes and dress in preventing sexual sin, men also have a responsibility. In 2 Timothy 2:22 Paul instructs Timothy to flee from lust. Men, when you see a provocatively dressed woman (in or out of the worship service), what's your reaction? Do you stare? Or can you say with Job, "I have made a covenant with my eyes; why then should I look upon a young woman" (Job 31:1, NKJV*)? Are you obeying Paul's command to flee from sexual sin, or are you courting it by reading books, looking at magazines, or watching TV programs and movies that you know are wrong? Memorize Job 31:1, 1 Corinthians 6:18, and 2 Timothy 2:22. Then put their teaching into practice by making yourself accountable to a spiritually mature brother in Christ for your thought life and your reading and viewing habits.

New King James Version.

2
God's High Calling for Women—Part 2

Outline

Introduction

Review
I. The Appearance of Women (v. 9*a*, *c*)
II. The Attitude of Women (v. 9*b*)

Lesson
III. The Testimony of Women (v. 10)
  A. The Importance of a Woman's Testimony
  B. The Desecration of a Woman's Testimony
  C. The Substance of a Woman's Testimony
IV. The Role of Women (vv. 11-12)
  A. In the Old Testament
    1. Their spiritual equality
      a) They had the same spiritual responsibilities as men
        (1) To obey the law
        (2) To teach the law
        (3) To participate in the festivals
      b) They had the same protection as men
      c) They took the same vows as men
      d) They had the same access to God as men
      e) They had the same privileges as men
    2. Their separate role
      a) They did not serve as leaders
      b) They had no ongoing prophetic ministry
        (1) Miriam
        (2) Deborah
        (3) Huldah
        (4) Noadiah
        (5) The wife of Isaiah

B. In the New Testament
   1. Their spiritual equality
      a) They had the same responsibilities as men
      b) They had the same access to Jesus as men
   2. Their separate role
      a) They did not serve as leaders
      b) They did not have an ongoing prophetic role

Conclusion

Introduction

One of the problems facing Timothy in the Ephesian church was that some women were usurping the role of men, desiring to be the official teachers. Other women were desecrating the worship service by coming with wrong attitudes and improper dress. Their behavior contradicted their profession to know and worship God. In 1 Timothy 2:9-15 Paul gives instruction on the role of women in the church—a topic relevant to today.

Review

I. THE APPEARANCE OF WOMEN (v. 9*a, c*; see pp. 11-15)

II. THE ATTITUDE OF WOMEN (v. 9*b*; see pp. 15-18)

Lesson

III. THE TESTIMONY OF WOMEN (v. 10)

"But (which becometh women professing godliness) with good works."

A. The Importance of a Woman's Testimony

Paul was concerned that a woman's testimony be consistent. The Greek word translated "professing" (*epangellō*) means "to make a public announcement." Any woman who has made a public announcement about her commitment to the Lord should conduct herself in a manner consistent with such a profession.

"Godliness" (Gk., *theosebeia*) has the basic meaning of reverence to God. When a person claims to be a Christian, he is claiming to worship and serve God. Any woman who claims to serve and worship God should conduct herself in godliness. To do otherwise would bring reproach on the name of Christ.

B. The Desecration of a Woman's Testimony

Verse 10 points out a major problem with the contemporary women's liberation movement in the church. A woman who wants to serve and honor God cannot show disregard for what He says in His Word about the role of women.

C. The Substance of a Woman's Testimony

The testimony of a woman professing godliness is a life of good works, for righteous deeds demonstrate the genuineness of her faith. The same is true for men.

IV. THE ROLE OF WOMEN (vv. 11-12)

"Let the women learn in silence with all subjection. But I permit not a woman to teach, nor to usurp authority over the man, but to be in silence."

The Greek word translated "learn" (*manthanō*) is in the imperative mood, indicating it is a command. Paul commanded that women be taught. Since this section of 1 Timothy is discussing how the church is to conduct itself (cf. 3:15), the learning is to take place when the church meets. We see from Acts 2:42 that learning was a high priority when the early church gathered together. Paul commanded that women be a part of the learning process. They were not to be excluded.

Women in First-Century Judaism

One of the problems in the Ephesian church was that some Jewish believers were still holding onto their Judaism. They were preoccupied with genealogies (1 Tim. 1:4), and some desired to be recognized as teachers of the law (1 Tim. 1:7). Part of contemporary Jewish tradition of that day was a low view of women. Women were not usually given opportunities to learn. They were not forbidden to come to the synagogue, but they were not encouraged to come, either. Most rabbis refused to greet women in public and believed that teaching them was a waste of time. Although women were not completely forbidden to learn, they were not encouraged to do so.

The Jewish view of teaching women no doubt led to a certain amount of suppression of women in the church at Ephesus. In reaction to that extreme position, some of the women determined to rise to the leadership level. First Timothy 2:12 says women were teaching and exercising authority over men. Paul told them to stop. But before Paul dealt with the problem of women's usurping the role of men, he first settled the question of whether women have a right to learn. His brief statement "let the women learn" shows there's equality of the sexes in spiritual life and blessing.

A. In the Old Testament

In spite of Jewish tradition, the Old Testament does not teach that women are inferior. The Old Testament teaches that women are spiritually equal to men.

1. Their spiritual equality

    a) They had the same responsibilities as men

    (1) To obey the law

        In Exodus 20 the Ten Commandments are given to both men and women. From the beginning, God laid down the principle that both men and women are responsible for obeying His laws.

(2) To teach the law

> Deuteronomy 6:6-7 says that both men and women are responsible to teach their children to obey God's law and to love Him. Proverbs 6:20 says, "My son, keep thy father's commandment, and forsake not the law of thy mother." The assumption is that both sexes are responsible to teach the law of God to their children, which means they must know the law of God.

(3) To participate in the festivals

> In Exodus 12 both men and women are involved in the Passover, one of the greatest celebrations of the Jewish calendar.

b) They had the same protection as men

Penalties given for crimes against women are the same as those for crimes against men (cf. Ex. 21:28-32). God values equally the life of a man and the life of a woman.

c) They took the same vows as men

The greatest vow an Israelite could take was the Nazirite vow. It was a vow of separation from the world and devotion to God. Women as well as men could take this vow (Num. 6:2). The highest level of spiritual commitment was not restricted to men.

d) They had the same access to God as men

God dealt directly with women in the Old Testament; He didn't go through men every time He wanted to communicate with them. For example, the angel of the Lord (a pre-incarnate manifestation of Christ) appeared to Hagar (Gen. 16:8-13) and the mother of Samson (Judg. 13:2-5).

e) They had the same privileges as men

Women as well as men served God in special ways. Nehemiah 7:67 tells of a choir made up of 245 singing men and women. They led the people to praise God through music. According to Exodus 38:8 women served at the door of the Tabernacle, possibly to instruct women who were coming to worship or to clean the Tabernacle grounds. From such passages as Deuteronomy 12:10-12, 1 Samuel 1, and 2 Samuel 6 we learn that women shared in the great national celebrations of Israel.

Thus, women had the same responsibility to obey the law and teach it to their children as did men. They participated in the religious life of Israel and served God. Far from giving women a secondary status, the Old Testament granted them spiritual equality with men.

2. Their separate role

Although women shared spiritual equality with men in the Old Testament, they did not have the same role. Nonetheless, that does not in any way diminish their spirituality.

a) They did not serve as leaders

There were no women rulers in the history of either Israel or Judah. Deborah was a judge who acted primarily in the role of an arbiter, not as an ongoing leader. That explains why she called on Barak when needing military leadership against the Canaanites (Judg. 4-5). Queen Athaliah was a usurper and not a legitimate ruler (2 Kings 11). There is no mention of women priests in the Old Testament. As far as we know, no woman wrote any portion of the Old Testament.

b) They had no ongoing prophetic ministry

No woman in Old Testament had an ongoing prophetic ministry such as that of Elisha or Elijah. There are five women in the Old Testament who are referred to as prophetesses.

(1) Miriam

Miriam was the sister of Moses and is called a prophetess in Exodus 15:20. Perhaps she is called a prophetess because she gives a brief revelation in verse 21. We know of no other occasion when she acted in the prophetic office.

(2) Deborah

Deborah is described as a prophetess in Judges 4:4 because she was used by God to give a direct revelation to Barak. We know of no other occasion when she engaged in ongoing prophetic work.

(3) Huldah

Huldah gave revelation from God to Hilkiah the priest and other men about the coming judgment on Jerusalem and Judah (2 Kings 22:14-22; 2 Chron. 34:22-28). There is no other recorded instance of her speaking as a prophetess.

(4) Noadiah

Noadiah was a false prophetess who opposed the work of Nehemiah in rebuilding the walls of Jerusalem (Neh. 6:14).

(5) The wife of Isaiah

Isaiah's wife is called a prophetess in Isaiah 8:3 because she gives birth to a child whose name had prophetic meaning. There is no record of her speaking a prophecy. This passage indicates that the word *prophetess* can be used in a general way.

The Old Testament differentiates the role of women from men. Women are not inferior to men but have a different role.

B. In the New Testament

1. Their spiritual equality

The spiritual equality of men and women is declared in Galatians 3:28: "There is neither Jew nor Greek, there is neither bond nor free, there is neither male nor female; for ye are all one in Christ Jesus." In the context of Galatians 3, the oneness spoken of here is the oneness of salvation. That is clear from verses 13-27. Paul's point is that all people—Jews and Gentiles, slaves and free men, men and women—have equal access to the salvation that is in Christ. The passage has nothing to do with the role of women in the church, nor does it teach that all differences are eliminated among Christians. A Jewish person did not cease to be Jewish when he became a Christian, and slaves did not automatically become free men. Some distinctions were retained.

a) They had the same spiritual responsibilities as men

All the commands, promises, and blessings of the New Testament are given equally to men and women. We all have the same spiritual resources and the same spiritual responsibilities.

b) They had the same access to Jesus as men

Jesus first revealed He was the Messiah to a woman (John 4). Jesus healed women (Matt. 8:14-15), showing them as much compassion as He did men. He taught women (Luke 10:38-42) and allowed them to minister to Him (Luke 8:3). At the cross, the women remained after the men had fled (Matt. 27:55-56). A woman first saw the resurrected Christ (Mark 16:9; John 20:11-18).

2. Their separate role

a) They did not serve as leaders

There is no record in the New Testament of a woman apostle, pastor, teacher, evangelist, or elder. The

28

New Testament does not record any sermon or teaching by a woman.

b) They did not have an ongoing prophetic role

Some argue that the daughters of Philip prophesied (Acts 21:9). However, they are not referred to as prophets, nor is there any indication of how often they prophesied. They may have spoken on only one occasion, as Deborah and Miriam apparently did in the Old Testament. The New Testament records other occasions when women spoke the word of God. Mary, the mother of Jesus, speaks the word of God in Luke 1:46-55. First Corinthians 11:5 says that women who prophesy are to have their heads covered. Acts 2:17 speaks of women prophesying. The Greek word translated "prophesy" simply means "to speak forth" or "to proclaim." There are times and places when women speak the word of God, but that is distinctly different from being identified as a pastor, teacher, elder, evangelist, or apostle.

Conclusion

Women have an important place in the plan of God, and they are equal with men spiritually. However, they are not to function in the same role as men. Because women are spiritually equal, Paul insisted that they be given the same opportunities to learn as men. Women cannot teach spiritual truths to their children (as Timothy's mother and grandmother did), lead people to Christ, or obey God if they are not given the opportunity to learn. Paul wanted to clearly teach that the differences in roles between men and women do not in any way imply the spiritual inferiority of women. He said, "Let the women *learn*" (v. 11, emphasis added).

Focusing on the Facts

1. What were some of the problems relating to women in the Ephesian church (see p. 22)?

2. Why is it important that a woman's testimony match her profession of faith (see pp. 22-23)?
3. The testimony of a woman professing godliness is a life of
   _____ _____ (see p. 23).
4. According to Acts 2:42, _____ was a high priority when the early church gathered together (see p. 23).
5. In your own words, summarize the place of women in first-century Judaism (see p. 24).
6. True or false: The contemporary Jewish view of women influenced the way women were being treated in the Ephesian church (see p. 24).
7. True or false: The Old Testament, in agreement with Jewish tradition, teaches that women are inferior spiritually (see p. 24).
8. Name some of the spiritual responsibilities women shared with men in the Old Testament (see pp. 24-25).
9. How did the role of women in the Old Testament differ from that of men (see pp. 26-27)?
10. Does Galatians 3:28 teach that all differences between men and women have been eliminated? Explain (see p. 28).
11. Did Jesus treat women as inferior to men? Support your answer from Scripture (see p. 28).
12. Why is it important for women to learn spiritual truth (see p. 29)?

Pondering the Principles

1. The church at Ephesus was influenced by the prevailing views of society regarding women. The same could be said about the church today. The church is often influenced *by* the world instead of being an influence *on* the world. Are your views shaped by the opinions of society or by God's Word? Think about your position on such issues as women's roles, abortion, homosexuality, creation and evolution, the Christian's responsibility to government, lawsuits, and divorce and remarriage. Spend time in prayer, and ask God to give you the courage to take a stand on these issues based on His Word—no matter what society propagates. Then pray that the church as a whole will also stand firm for God's truth.

2. Jesus ministered to all types of people, even those His culture considered inferior. He ministered to the poor, lepers, and tax collectors. Are you selective about whom you allow yourself to

get involved with? Do you reach out to the difficult people and strangers at your church and Bible study group, or do you play it safe and stick with your friends? The next time you see a person in need and are tempted to turn away because he isn't part of your crowd, remember the example of Jesus as well as the teaching in James 2:1-9.

3
God's High Calling for Women—Part 3

Outline

Introduction

Review
I. The Appearance of Women (v. 9*a*, *c*)
II. The Attitude of Women (v. 9*b*)
III. The Testimony of Women (v. 10)
IV. The Role of Women (vv. 11-12)
  A. In the Old Testament
  B. In the New Testament

Lesson
  C. In the Church
    1. They are to learn in silence (v. 11*a*; 1 Cor. 14:34)
      a) The reason for women's silence
      b) The meaning of women's silence
        (1) The corruption
        (2) The correction
        (3) The concession
    2. They are to learn in subjection (v. 11*b*; 1 Cor. 11:3)
      a) The source of subjection
      b) The symbols of subjection
      c) The significance of subjection

Introduction

Catharine Beecher was the oldest child in her family. One of her younger sisters was novelist Harriet Beecher Stowe, author of *Uncle Tom's Cabin*. Catharine grew up with a great love for children, finding joy in rearing and caring for them. Her mother was a skilled homemaker and taught her how to take care of the home.

When Catharine was sixteen her mother died, and an aunt moved in. Her aunt was noted for her neatness and ability to manage the home orderly and economically. Catharine's father eventually remarried, and her step-mother was also an expert homemaker. Catharine, under the tutelage of those exemplary women, decided in turn to train other women for their domestic responsibilities. At the age of twenty-three she founded The Hartford Female Seminary, which trained women to be lovers of their husbands and children and keepers of the home.

In 1869 Catharine and Harriet wrote a book entitled *The American Woman's Home* (New York: J. B. Ford). They wrote, "Woman's profession embraces the care and nursing of the body in the critical periods of infancy and sickness, the training of the human mind in the most impressionable period of childhood . . . and most of the government and economies of the family state. These duties of woman are as sacred and important as any ordained to man; and yet no such advantages for preparation have been accorded her, nor is there any qualified body to certify the public that a woman is duly prepared to give proper instruction in her profession" (p. 14). It was their desire to train women "not only to perform in the most approved manner all the manual employments of domestic life, but to honor and enjoy these duties" (pp. 14-15).

If a woman today were to establish a female seminary to train women in domestic responsibilities, she would become the laughingstock of the Western world. Training women to keep the home opposes what society teaches is important.

Review

In 1 Timothy 2:9-15 Paul gives us a comprehensive treatment of the role of women in the church.

I. THE APPEARANCE OF WOMEN (v. 9*a*, *c*; see pp. 11-15)

II. THE ATTITUDE OF WOMEN (v. 9*b*; see pp. 15-18)

III. THE TESTIMONY OF WOMEN (v. 10; see pp. 22-23)

IV. THE ROLE OF WOMEN (vv. 11-12)

"Let the women learn in silence with all subjection. But I permit not a woman to teach, nor to usurp authority over the man, but to be in silence."

A. In the Old Testament (see pp. 24-27)

B. In the New Testament (see pp. 28-29)

Lesson

C. In the Church

> **The Role of Women in Greek Society**
>
> The church at Ephesus existed in a city dominated by Greek culture and religion. According to William Barclay, "The place of women in Greek religion was low. The Temple of Aphrodite in Corinth had a thousand priestesses who were sacred prostitutes and every evening plied their trade on the city streets. The Temple of Diana in Ephesus had its hundreds of priestesses called the *Melissae*, which means the *bees*, whose function was the same. The respectable Greek woman led a very confined life. She lived in her own quarters into which no one but her husband came. She did not even appear at meals. She never at any time appeared on the street alone; she never went to any public assembly. The fact is that if in a Greek town Christian women had taken an active and a speaking part in its work, the Church would inevitably have gained the reputation of being the resort of loose women" (*The Letters to Timothy, Titus, and Philemon*, rev. ed. [Philadelphia: Westminster, 1975], p. 67).

Paul makes two points in verse 11 about women in the church: they are to learn in silence, and they are to learn in submission. The Greek word translated "silence" (*hēsuchia*) means silence. We'll have to determine its exact meaning from the context. The Greek word translated "subjection" is from *hupotassō*, which means "to line up under." Women are not to be rebels; they're to be in their proper place.

The instruction for women's silence has been misinterpreted in two ways. Those who believe women are free to preach in the church interpret "silence" as a reference to a meek and quiet spirit. They say that this passage says women preachers or teachers are to have meek and quiet demeanors. Others go to the opposite extreme and insist that no woman should ever speak in church under any circumstance—not even to the person she is sitting next to. However, Paul in verse 12 says women are to be silent in the sense of not teaching or exercising authority over men in the church.

1. They are to learn in silence (v. 11*a*; 1 Cor. 14:34)

"Let the women learn in silence."

1 Corinthians 14:34 echoes the thought of 1 Timothy 2:11. Paul wrote, "Let your women keep silence in the churches; for it is not permitted unto them to speak, but they are commanded to be under obedience, as also saith the law."

a) The reason for women's silence

The reason women are not to preach in the church has nothing to do with their psychological makeup or intellectual capabilities. The last phrase in 1 Corinthians 14:34 says women are not to teach in the church because God's law forbids it (cf. Gen. 3:16).

b) The meaning of women's silence

The context of 1 Corinthians 14 indicates that the silence Paul commands is not intended to preclude women from speaking at all but to keep them from speaking in tongues and prophesying in the church.

The Spectacle of the Oracle

The city of Delphi, located across the Gulf of Corinth, was the seat of a religion headed by a woman known as the Pythia, or the oracle of Delphi. To qualify for the office of priestess in this religion, a woman had to be a young virgin. Later, married women over fifty were preferred, but they were required to dress like maidens. Each priestess was a medium in contact with demon spirits.

A man desiring to consult the oracle (no women were allowed to consult) sacrificed an animal while a few attendant priestesses evaluated the omens. If they were favorable, the man was permitted to enter the inner shrine. After entering he wrote his request on a tablet (archaeologists have excavated the shrine area and found some of those tablets still intact), which would probably then be read to the Pythia. The Pythia sat on a tripod, allegedly over a chasm from which a mystic vapor from the ground arose. Before taking her seat, she drank water from the prophetic stream called Kassotis and ate sacred laurel leaves. In response to the question on the tablet, she uttered incoherent sounds that were interpreted (often in perfect hexameter verse) by a male prophet who stood nearby. The interpretation, which was often obscure and variable, usually left the inquirer more mystified than when he came.

That pagan practice had a negative impact on the church at Corinth. Some people came into the Corinthian assembly and uttered similar ecstatic speech, supposedly in the power of the Holy Spirit. That led to chaos in the Corinthian church. The true gifts of speaking in tongues and prophesying became confused with satanic counterfeits.

(1) The corruption

At Corinth, as in Ephesus, women flaunted their sexuality. Perhaps influenced by the Delphic religion, they sought prominent positions in the Corinthian church by abusing the gifts of speaking in tongues and prophesying.

(2) The correction

In response to that problem Paul wrote, "How is it, then, brethren? When ye come together, every one of you hath a psalm, hath a doctrine, hath a tongue, hath a revelation, hath an interpretation. Let all things be done unto edifying" (1 Cor. 14:26). Paul went on to say that no more than two or three were to speak in tongues and never without an interpreter present. Only two or three prophets were to speak, and others were to evaluate them to see if they spoke the truth (vv. 27-29). Paul's point was that God is not the author of confusion (v. 33). Finally, Paul instructed the women to keep silent (v. 34). They were not to speak in tongues or prophesy in the public assembly of the church.

First Timothy 2:11-12 and 1 Corinthians 14:34-35 tell us that when the church comes together, women are not to speak in tongues, prophesy, or teach the Word of God. When the church comes together the appointed men are to do the teaching.

(3) The concession

That doesn't mean women can never speak God's truth. God used women such as Miriam (Ex. 15:20-21), Deborah (Judges 4:4), Huldah (2 Kings 22:14-22), and Anna (Luke 2:36-38) to speak for Him. Paul spoke with various churches and synagogues during his missionary journeys, answering questions from women as well as men (cf. Acts 17:2-4). I believe there is a time and place for women to publicly offer a testimony of praise to the Lord. I don't believe Paul is saying women can never do that. But he forbade women to take leadership roles in the church.

2. They are to learn in subjection (v. 11b; 1 Cor. 11:3)

"Let the women learn . . . with all subjection."

In 1 Corinthians 11:3 Paul says, "The head of every man is Christ; and the head of the woman is the man; and the head of Christ is God." That verse teaches that women are to be in submission to men in the sense that they are not to usurp the role of leadership in the church, which belongs to qualified men.

a) The source of subjection

No believer argues that Christ is not the head of man. And believers understand that God the Father is the head of Christ. Philippians 2:5-8 teaches that Christ took upon Himself the form of a servant during His incarnation. Since Christ is the head of the man and God the Father is the head of Christ, why do we debate about whether the man is the head of the woman?

b) The symbols of subjection

In Corinth it was customary for married women to cover their heads to display their modesty. It was a sign that they were committed to their husbands and not available. Men, on the other hand, had their heads uncovered as a mark of their masculinity. In the Corinthian church those cultural signs were becoming inverted: women were praying and prophesying with their heads uncovered—thus identifying themselves with the liberated women in Corinth —and the men—perhaps because of Jewish influence—were covering their heads while praying. Paul rebukes the men in verse 4: "Every man praying or prophesying, having his head covered, dishonoreth his head." Does that mean it's a sin for men to have something on their heads when they pray? No, not unless your culture perceives that as something feminine. In verse 5 Paul rebukes the women: "Every woman that prayeth or prophesieth with her head uncovered dishonoreth her head, for that is even all one as if she were shaved" (a shaved head was a symbol of shame).

We should identify with our society's symbols of masculinity and femininity unless they violate Scripture or God's design for morality. Such symbols in our society can be readily discerned. We can tell the difference between a woman who looks like a woman and a woman who looks like she is rebelling against womanhood. We can look at a man and tell by the way he dresses and carries himself if he is denying the cultural symbols of masculinity.

Does 1 Corinthians 11:5 Permit Women Preachers?

Some people teach that the praying and prophesying of the women in 1 Corinthians 11:5 took place during the worship service. However, the text doesn't say that. Perhaps Paul was speaking of prayer and prophecy in general. It's not until verse 18 that Paul first speaks of the formal gathering of the church: "First of all, when ye come together in the church, I hear that there are divisions among you." Prior to verse 18 he apparently was not speaking of the worship service.

Perhaps Paul is speaking in verse 5 of women praying and proclaiming the Word of God in a home Bible study or family prayer time. His point was that whenever Christians get together, the women are to maintain the decorum of submission, and the men are to maintain the role of headship. If a woman was veiled when she prayed or spoke the Word of God, she attested to her womanhood and affirmed her submission to her husband. She was acknowledging that man is the image and glory of God and that she is the glory of man (v. 7). Man is symbolic of the glorious dominion of God, and woman is symbolic of the one who follows.

c) The significance of subjection

God designed human life to revolve around relationships. And within those relationships are differing roles. However, in our society we emphasize the individual over the relationship. Individuals focus on their rights, and they seek to satisfy themselves. In such a society there is a tendency to view everyone as having an equal role. But when women refuse to accept their God-ordained roles in the church and family, they undermine the foundational design of God for those institutions, and the stability of the society is at stake.

Some Practical Considerations

1. When can women proclaim the Word of God?

Women can proclaim the Word of God at any time and at any place, except when the church comes together for the worship service. The New Testament gives examples of Mary and Anna speaking the truth (Luke 1:46-55; 2:36-38).

2. In Bible studies, can women share what they've learned?

Yes, in the right environment there is nothing wrong with a woman's sharing what the Spirit of God has taught her out of the Word.

3. Can women pray in public?

Yes, women can pray in public. Acts 1:13-14 describes a prayer meeting where the disciples of Jesus as well as several women were present. There is a time and a place when it is perfectly appropriate for a woman to pray in public.

When Paul writes in 1 Timothy 2:11, "Let the woman learn in silence," he means that women are not to teach during the official meeting of the church. The responsibility of being the preacher, the teacher, or the one who leads in prayer in the worship service is a role ordained for men.

Focusing on the Facts

1. The city of Ephesus was dominated by _____ culture and religion (see p. 35).
2. True or false: Women enjoyed a great amount of personal freedom in Greek society, often taking an active role in the public assemblies (see p. 35).
3. What two points does Paul make in 1 Timothy 2:11 about the role of women in the church (see p. 35)?
4. True or false: Paul's command that women keep silent in the church means that a woman is not to speak under any circumstances (see p. 36).
5. What is the reason women are not permitted to teach in the church (see p. 36)?
6. Describe the influence the Delphic religion had on the Corinthian church (see pp. 36-37).
7. How did Paul instruct the Corinthians to correct the problems in their church (see pp. 37-38)?
8. Why was it wrong for the Corinthian men to pray with their heads covered (see p. 39)?

9. Does 1 Corinthians 11:5 teach that women can proclaim God's Word in the church service? Support your answer (see pp. 39-40).
10. Why is it such a serious matter for women to reject the roles God has designed for them in the family and the church (see p. 40)?

Pondering the Principles

1. Some women in the Ephesian and Corinthian churches were more concerned with their rights than with their responsibilities to God and the church. What about you? Is your focus on getting or giving? Do you more frequently demand your rights or fulfill your responsibilities? Remember that Jesus came not "to be served, but to serve" (Matt. 20:28, NASB*). If your focus has gradually changed from ministering to the needs of others to looking out for your own rights, you can help get it back where it belongs by memorizing Philippians 2:3-4.

2. We've learned in this chapter that both men and women can (under the right circumstances) proclaim God's truth. Do you regularly look for opportunities to share the truths of Scripture with your friends? your neighbors? your spouse? your children? To communicate the truths of the Bible we must first learn them ourselves. That requires constant study. If you aren't regularly studying Scripture, make a commitment to the Lord to begin today.

*New American Standard Bible.

4
God's High Calling for Women—Part 4

Outline

Introduction

Review
I. The Appearance of Women (v. 9a, c)
II. The Attitude of Women (v. 9b)
III. The Testimony of Women (v. 10)
IV. The Role of Women (vv. 11-12)
   A. In the Old Testament
   B. In the New Testament
   C. In the Church
      1. They are to learn in silence (v. 11a)
      2. They are to learn in subjection (v. 11b)

Lesson
      3. They are not to teach (v. 12a)
      4. They are not to usurp authority (v. 12b)
         a) What that means
         b) What that does not mean
V. The Design of Women (vv. 13-14)
   A. Established by the Creation (v. 13)
   B. Confirmed by the Fall (v. 14)
VI. The Contribution of Women (v. 15)
   A. Women's Salvation Defined
   B. Women's Significance Delineated

Conclusion

Introduction

When Paul says farewell to the elders of the Ephesian church in Acts 20, he warns them that false teachers will arise within the church as well as outside (Acts 20:29-30). Tragically, Paul's fears for the Ephesian church were realized. In part, Paul wrote his first letter to Timothy to deal with the false leaders who were plaguing the church at Ephesus.

One of the false teachings concerned the role of women. Errant leaders were advocating an unbiblical role for women. In fact, it is possible that some of those leaders were themselves women. Paul makes six points in 1 Timothy 2:9-15 to set forth the biblical role for women in the church.

Review

3. They are not to teach (v. 12*a*)

"I permit not a woman to teach."

"Permit" means to allow someone to do what he wants. By his word choice, Paul implied that some women at Ephesus had the desire to lead the church. There have always been women who seek leadership roles. Genesis 3:15-16 suggests that part of the result of the Fall was that the woman would desire to control the man, and the man would have to rule over her. The Hebrew word translated "desire" in Genesis 3:16 is used only one other time in the Pentateuch, where it speaks of the desire of sin to control Cain (cf. Gen. 4:7). We can conclude from that usage that Genesis 3:16 is saying women desire to take the control from men.

There are women in the church who are not content with their God-given role. They seek a place of prominence by exercising authority over men. Paul forbade women from taking the authoritative pastor-teacher role in the church. No woman is presented in such an office in the New Testament.

4. They are not to usurp authority (v. 12*b*)

"Nor to usurp authority over the man, but to be in silence."

a) What that means

"Usurp authority" (Gk., *authentein*) is used only here in the New Testament. A study of that verb by George Knight concluded that the common meaning of *authentein* in extrabiblical literature is "to have authority over" ("*Authenteō* in Reference to Women in 1 Timothy 2:12," *New Testament Studies*, vol. 30 [1984]: 143-57). He discovered no negative connotation such as "abusing authority."

b) What that does not mean

    (1) That women are not to take abusive authority

        Some people have reinterpreted *authentein* in 1 Timothy 2:12 to mean "abusive authority." They believe it is acceptable for women to teach and exercise authority over men as long as their authority does not become abusive. However, *authentein* does not mean "abusive authority." There's no justification for that addition to the text. If Paul were speaking of abusive authority, he would not have limited his warning to women.

        Teaching and usurping authority contrast with silence and subjection. Women in the church are not to be in any position where men are subordinate to them.

    (2) That women are not permitted to pray

        The phrase "be in silence" in verse 12 is not intended to prohibit women from praying. It teaches that just as women are not to function in the office of teacher or leader in the church, so they are not to lead in the public prayer time of the church.

    (3) That women are never to teach

        There is a time and place for women to instruct. Under some circumstances a woman, along with her husband, could instruct another man. Priscilla and Aquila instructed Apollos (Acts 18:26). However, such instruction would not take place in the public worship service of the church.

    (4) That women do not have spiritual gifts

        Women can have the same spiritual gifts men have, including the gifts of teaching and leadership. The Lord gives women ample opportunity to use those gifts in a setting that doesn't violate His designed role for them. Women can use those gifts in situations apart from the worship service of the church. A woman is in no way wronged in being limited to her God-ordained role in the church and not being permitted to usurp the role of a man. There's plenty of opportunity for women to exercise their gifts in a manner consistent with God's design.

(5) That women cannot serve as missionaries

I thank God for the many faithful women who serve on the mission field. However, I don't believe women on the mission field have the right to violate their God-ordained role. Paul himself was a missionary. If there was ever a need for leadership on the mission field, it was in his day. Paul could have compromised by using women in leadership roles, but he didn't. When there is a shortage of men on a mission field, the answer is not to violate biblical principles but to pray for the Lord of the harvest to send forth more workers (Matt. 9:38).

Elisabeth Elliot, after the murder of her husband, Jim, and several other missionaries in Ecuador, was the only missionary left who could speak the language of the Auca Indians. She taught one of the Auca men the sermon each week, and he then preached it to the church.

(6) That women are inferior

Women are not inferior to men; they simply have a different role. Many people believe that the only place of power and influence is in a leadership role. They believe it is more fulfilling to lead than to follow. But people in non-leadership roles can be significantly influential as well.

The role of subordination and subjection often brings the greatest peace, happiness, and contentment. The idea that the greatest experience in life is to be on top of the pile and control everything is an illusion. I advise any woman who desires to be a leader in the church to stay under the loving care and protection of her husband and the current church leaders. It's a happier place to be; the burden is significantly lighter. Subjection is not a punishment; it is a privilege.

V. THE DESIGN OF WOMEN (vv. 13-14)

A. Established by the Creation (v. 13)

"For Adam was first formed, then Eve."

Woman's subordinate role was ordained in the order of the creation. Adam was created first, then Eve. In 1 Corinthians 11:8-9 Paul writes, "The man is not of the woman, but the woman of the man. Neither was the man created for the woman, but the woman for the man." She was made to be his helper (Gen. 2:18). She was to follow his lead, live on his provisions, and find safety in his strength and protection through his courage. The tendency to follow was built into Eve, but with the Fall came conflict.

The subordinate role of women is not a cultural issue. It cannot be explained as mere bias on Paul's part, because it is based on the order of creation. Adam was first formed, then Eve.

B. Confirmed by the Fall (v. 14)

"Adam was not deceived, but the woman, being deceived, was in the transgression."

When we think about the Fall, we usually think of it in connection with Adam. Romans 5:12-21 speaks repeatedly of the one man (Adam) who brought sin and death into the world. Adam bears responsibility for the Fall since he is the head of the human race. But we have to keep in mind that he didn't fall first—Eve did. When Eve got out from under the protection of Adam's leadership and attempted to deal independently with the enemy, she was deceived. That reinforces the truth that women were designed with the need for a leader.

48

Eve showed by the fact she was deceived that she was unable to lead effectively. She met her match in Satan. The Greek word translated "deceived" (*exapataō*) in verse 14 is a strong term. It is stronger than the common Greek word for "deceived" (*apataō*). It refers to being thoroughly deceived. And so we conclude that when a woman leaves the shelter of her protector she has a certain amount of vulnerability.

The Fall was the result not only of disobeying God's command but also of violating the divinely appointed role of the sexes. Eve acted independently and assumed the role of leadership. Adam violated his role by abdicating his leadership position and following Eve's lead. Nevertheless, it is important to note that women are not more defective than men. And just as women need men, so men need women. We're all vulnerable in different ways.

We affirm the leadership of men because it is established by the creation and confirmed by the Fall. And no daughter of Eve should follow her path and enter into the forbidden territory of rulership that was intended for men.

VI. THE CONTRIBUTION OF WOMEN (v. 15)

"Notwithstanding, she shall be saved in childbearing, if they continue in faith and love and holiness with sobriety."

In verse 14 we read of woman's being in sin. In contrast, verse 15 speaks of women being saved through childbearing. The salvation spoken of is not salvation from sin. And it cannot refer to Eve since the future tense is used—"she shall be saved." Furthermore, the use of the plural pronoun *they* indicates that more than one woman is in view. It clearly indicates that all women are in view here.

A. Women's Salvation Defined

The Greek word translated "saved" (*sōzō*) can refer to being saved from things other than sin. This verse is saying that through childbearing all women are delivered from the stigma of a woman's originating the Fall. A woman led the human race into sin, yet women benefit mankind by replenishing it. They also have the opportunity to lead the race to godliness through their influence on children.

B. Women's Significance Delineated

A mother's godliness and virtue can have a profound impact on the life of her children. The rearing of children gives a woman dignity. Her great contribution comes in motherhood. However, she must continue in faith, love, and holiness. Only a godly mother can rear godly children.

Obviously, God doesn't want all women to be mothers. Some of them He doesn't even want to be married, since according to 1 Corinthians 7 some have the gift of singleness. Others He allows to be barren for His own purposes. But as a general rule, motherhood is the greatest contribution a woman can make to the human race. The pain of childbearing was woman's punishment for sin, but bearing and rearing children delivers woman from the stigma of that sin.

Conclusion

Paul, under the inspiration of the Holy Spirit, says women are to accept their God-given role. They must not seek the leadership role in the church. Primarily they are to raise godly children. How tragic that so many women feel their lives are unfulfilled because they can't function in the same roles as men. Yet God has given them the unique privilege of rearing a godly generation of children—and of having an intimate relationship with them that no father can know.

Portrait of a Godly Mother

Susanna Wesley has gone down in history as one of the greatest Christian mothers. She was the wife of a pastor and the mother of nineteen children. Only about half of those children survived infancy. Two of her sons were John and Charles Wesley, who helped bring revival to England while France was bathed in bloody revolution. Susanna spent one hour each day alone with God in her room, praying for each of her children.

1. What was one of the reasons Paul wrote 1 Timothy (see p. 44)?
2. What was one of the teachings that the false leaders were advocating (see p. 44)?
3. The conflict of the sexes was one of the results of _____ _____ (see p. 45).
4. True or false: No woman is ever seen in the role of pastor-teacher in the New Testament (see p. 45).
5. True or false: The Greek word *authentein* is used frequently in the New Testament to refer to abusive authority (see p. 45).
6. What restrictions are placed on a woman's use of her spiritual gifts (see pp. 46-47)?
7. What should be done on the mission field when there is a shortage of men for leadership (see p. 47)?
8. True or false: Women are not to function in leadership roles because they are inferior to men (see p. 47).
9. Subjection is not a _____; it's a _____ (see p. 48).
10. Why can't Paul's teaching on the subordination of women be dismissed as a cultural bias (see p. 48)?
11. In what sense is a woman saved in childbearing (see pp. 49-50)?
12. Why can't 1 Timothy 2:15 refer to Eve or Mary? To whom does it refer (see p. 49)?
13. True or false: God wants all women to be mothers (see p. 50).

Pondering the Principles

1. Christians today tend to compromise biblical teaching and standards. Under pressure from the feminist movement, some Christians have reinterpreted the Bible's teaching on the role of women. Others have reinterpreted the first few chapters of Genesis in a futile attempt to harmonize the account of creation with the pseudo-science of evolution. Some insist that the Bible does not teach all the principles necessary to address life's problems. The faith "once for all delivered to the saints" (Jude 3, NASB) has too often become like a weather vane—shifting with each passing wind of change. What is the ultimate source of authority in your life? When faced with a conflict between biblical teaching and a contemporary idea, what do you do? Do you reinterpret

the Bible or reject the idea? Are you willing to take a stand for God's Word? Study Psalm 19:7-11 to see how God describes His Word, and determine to uphold it.

2. Husbands, how well are you performing your role as your wife's protector? Do you protect her from physical and emotional harm, or do you physically or emotionally abuse her—or let your children do so? Do you do everything in your power to protect her holiness and purity, or do you allow her to be exposed to compromising situations? Do you lead by being a sacrificial servant or a despotic dictator? Do you make your wife's submission to you a heavy burden for her to bear? Examine the quality of your love for your wife by comparing it with the way Christ loves the church. You might wish to begin by meditating on Ephesians 5:25-29.

Scripture Index

Topical Index

Moody Press, a ministry of the Moody Bible Institute, is designed for education, evangelization, and edification. If we may assist you in knowing more about Christ and the Christian life, please write us without obligation: Moody Press, c/o MLM, Chicago, Illinois 60610.